# LILY LEAVES
# SLOANE SQUARE

For Olivia, who always loves my stories

Lily Leaves Sloane Square
Written by SungHee Lim

ISBN: 979-8-865059-36-3

First Edition: November 2023

This book belongs to

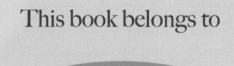

_____

This is Sloane Square.
Many people bustle through this station every day, rain or shine.

However, no one notices something special about this station!

There is someone special who was born here and has been living in the station her entire life without setting foot outside.

This is Lily. She is a city frog.

Although, she's never been outside of Sloane Square.
So maybe she is a station frog.

Lily is a very happy station frog.
She dances like no one is watching when
she feels stuck.

She runs around like she's got wings on
her feet, catching flies when she's feeling
hungry.

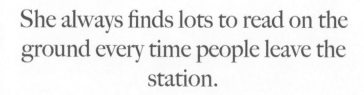

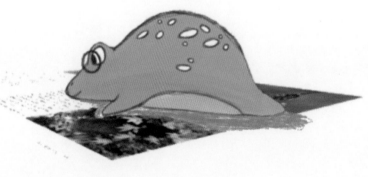

She always finds lots to read on the
ground every time people leave the
station.

One very ordinary, dreary London afternoon, Lily noticed something moving on the wall. She got close to see what it was. It had a very small head and eight extra lanky legs!

"Hey! You're Mr. Peter, the friendly neighbourhood spider!" Lily exclaimed.

"Hello!" said the spider. "Yes, I guess once you help out some bees, everyone knows who you are! Those bees are always buzzing and talking!" he rambled on, with a bit of a sigh.

Mr. Peter just kept talking, describing his daily adventures out above the station...where 'the real Sloan Square' is.

He described busy streets filled with people, cars, and tall trees that touch the sky because no one can see the tip of them.

Mr. Peter also spoke of a big ocean that people called a fountain.

Mr. Peter told Lily how bizarre it was to see dogs who had their humans tied to them…like they would lose their humans if they just let them wander freely!

Everything Mr. Peter was saying sounded nothing like Lily had ever seen or heard before. Lily felt the heavy thumping of her heart as she imagined life above the station. Lily began to shout over and over "I will come with you! I will come with you!"

"Great!" said Mr. Peter.
"Maybe you can warn me
of snail trails. I do not like stepping
on those!" he rumbled under his breath,
as he agreed to take Lily on his daily adventure.

"First, we have to wait for the sun to come out. You see, there's an old spider's tale about going up anywhere on rainy days. There once was a great, brave spider who decided to climb up for the first time ever in the history of all spiders" he continued.

"He picked the world's tallest water spout to climb up. But every time rain comes, a flood of water would wash him down! That's how spiders got wise about water. You have to stay away from the rain," Mr. Peter explained, as he started singing an old spider folk song.

As Mr. Peter crawled up the wall, Lily followed right behind him. Well, she tried to follow…but she couldn't! Every time Lily tried to climb the wall, she would fall!

Mr. Peter had already made it to the top. Looking down at Lily, he sighed. "Well, I have important spider stuff to do up here and can't wait for you. Just keep trying. And remember, only climb up when the sun is out!" Mr. Peter shouted from the top as he trotted away.

All of a sudden the typical dreary London sky returned. It was dark, and the air began to feel wet.

Drip, drip, drip-drop, Lily felt the water start to come down from up top. It was that dangerous rain Mr. Peter warned her about!

Lily tried to protect herself from the rain. She didn't want to get wet! She thought it would only make it harder for her to climb up later. So Lily just sat there, waiting for the rain to stop.

As Lily sat there, a bird swooped in with a puzzled look on its face. "I have been watching you try to climb up the wall, frog" said the bird.

"Oh yes", sighed Lily. "I am trying to go on an adventure above the station. But I can't seem to figure out how to climb the wall."

Lily continued, "Mr. Peter the spider told me to never try when it's raining. When the sun is out, he just climbs up the wall so quickly!"

Curiously, the bird said, "Hmm, I've flown around the world from up high, rain or shine, kid. I've made plenty of mistakes along the way."

"Something I've learned that you should remember...what works for someone else might not work for you! You gotta find your own way" said the bird.

Lily, inspired by the bird's words of wisdom, thought long and hard before deciding to try again. This time, Lily chose a path that was different from Mr. Peter's way and felt more natural to her.

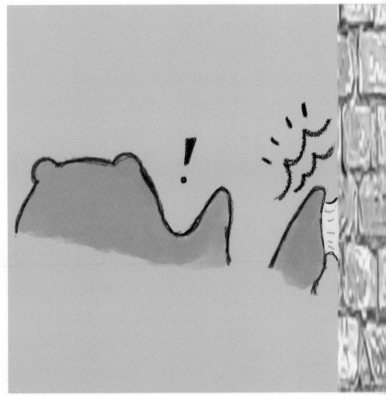

Lily put her leaf down, walked to the wall in the rain and touched it. "Wait...WHAT?! What is this sticky feeling?" she shouted. Lily couldn't believe how sticky the wall was!

Feeling confident, Lily started to climb with her hands and feet,
one step at a time. She felt more stuck to the wall than ever!
Quickly, Lily made it to the top of the brick wall
just as the rain stopped.

When she arrived at the top, her mouth dropped to the floor
as she looked out from above the wall.

She couldn't believe her eyes!

As Lily stood there, excited for her adventure, Mr. Peter trotted over. "Ah! You are one of those rainy day sticky fellas!" he muttered, with a smile on his face.

The bird, who had inspired Lily to find her own way, flew up from the station, landing next to them and said, "You see, what works for your friends might not work for you. Sometimes there is more than one way to make something work."

"We all have different stories to tell, we have our own strengths, and we can all be there for each other to help friends find their own way" said the mysterious bird.

"Wow! You are so wise!" exclaimed Lily.
"Thank you...what is your name?" she asked.

"Oh. I guess I should have introduced myself. My name is John.
But most people call me P. John."

The End